ON OUR KNEES

A PRAYER JOURNAL

ON OUR KNEES

A PRAYER JOURNAL

PHIL WICKHAM

WITH MATT LITTON

K-LOVE BOOKS

FRANKLIN, TENNESSEE

K-LOVE BOOKS
5700 West Oaks Blvd
Rocklin, CA 95765

Printed in the United States of America.

First edition: 2023
10 9 8 7 6 5 4 3 2 1

ISBN: 978-1-954201-54-5 (Hardcover)
ISBN: 978-1-954201-55-2 (E-book)

Publisher's Cataloging-in-Publication Data

Names: Wickham, Phil, author. | Litton, Matt, author.
Title: On our knees : a prayer journal / Phil Wickham; with Matt Litton.
Description: Nashville: Dexterity Collective, 2023.
Identifiers: ISBN: 978-1-954201-54-5 (hardcover) | 978-1-954201-55-2 (ebook)
Subjects: LCSH Prayer--Christianity. | Devotional calendars. | BISAC RELIGION / Christian Living / Prayer | RELIGION / Christian Living / Devotional Journal
Classification: LCC BV4811 .W53 2023 | DDC 242.2--dc23

Cover design by Bruce Gore
Interior design by PerfecType, Nashville, TN

CONTENTS

CONTENTS

CONTENTS

INTRODUCTION

How to Use This Prayer Journal

The writing of *On Our Knees: 40 Days to Living Boldly in Prayer* came from the simple desire to grow deeper in my faith. I set out to learn more about the practice, the power, and the joy of prayer by simply opening the Bible from Genesis on and discovering the beautiful lessons contained in God's great love story. I am still on the journey of learning how to live my life with a posture of prayer and an open heart. I have been moved to hear so many readers are experiencing God's call to move deeper into a life of prayer. As I continue to learn more about prayer, I've discovered that each time I think I am swimming in the deep end, God seems to lead me into even deeper waters. I have found that keeping a prayer journal has become a helpful tool as He teaches me more about prayer in my daily time with Him.

I want to offer you this journal to use in your own prayer time. It can be used as a companion to the *On Our Knees* devotional, but it is designed to be a meaningful prayer tool by itself. Each day in this prayer journal includes a Scripture reading from the devotional. It is offered so you can pray through the words of the Bible. This is an ancient Christian practice that has come to mean so much to me. It is called *lectio divina*, which simply means praying the words of the Bible. I am amazed at how often these moments of praying God's Word delivers just what I need most from Him. The journal provides space for you to write and reflect on how God speaks to you as you pray the Scripture.

Each day also provides a section to record your thanksgiving and praise. I am continually learning the importance of beginning prayer by considering God's goodness and His blessings. Each day you can write down the gifts in your life, your gratitude to Him, and the many reasons you have to praise Him.

The journal provides space to keep track of your petitions to God. Philippians 4:6 reminds us that we should bring *everything* before God in prayer. The battle belongs to Him, and I've found it humbling and encouraging to return to these prayer requests to find them answered. He is faithful!

Finally, so many readers have expressed that the daily prayer practice from *On Our Knees* was a meaningful part of the devotional. I have included some questions that can challenge you to go deeper into that day's prayer practice.

It is my sincerest hope this journal can become a helpful addition to your daily prayer time and will bring you closer to God as you grow further on this spiritual journey.

Sincerely,
Phil

DAY 1

PRAYER IS INTIMACY WITH GOD

PRAYER READING (*LECTIO DIVINA*): Genesis 1–3

As you read and thoughtfully pray through today's selected Scripture, ask God to point out what He wants to teach you from His Word.

> *God created mankind in his own image, in the image of God he created them; male and female he created them. God blessed them and said to them, "Be fruitful and increase in number; fill the earth and subdue it. Rule over the fish in the sea and the birds in the sky and over every living creature that moves on the ground."* **(Genesis 1:27–28)**

> *The* L*ORD* *God formed a man from the dust of the ground and breathed into his nostrils the breath of life, and the man became a living being. Now the* L*ORD* *God had planted a garden in the east, in Eden; and there he put the man he had formed.* **(Genesis 2:7–8)**
>
> *The man and his wife heard the sound of the* L*ORD* *God as he was walking in the garden in the cool of the day.* **(Genesis 3:8)**

Spend some time writing and reflecting about what spoke to you in today's prayer reading.

DAY 1

THANKSGIVING AND PRAISE

Before you pray, spend some time listing what you are thankful for today and the ways that God is good.

PRAYER REQUESTS

What are the needs in your life, in your family, in your community, and in the world that you need to bring to God today? Make a list of those needs, and spend some time bringing each request before Him.

PRAYER PRACTICE REFLECTION

Today's prayer practice challenged you to find time to go on a short walk and simply talk to God. What are a few ways that today's practice can affect your actions? What did it teach you about prayer?

DAY 1

DAY 2

GOD HEARS US . . . EVEN WHEN WE CAN'T PRAY WORDS!

PRAYER READING (*LECTIO DIVINA*): Exodus 2

As you read and thoughtfully pray through today's selected Scripture, ask God to point out what He wants to teach you from His Word.

> *During that long period, the king of Egypt died. The Israelites groaned in their slavery and cried out, and their cry for help because of their slavery went up to God. God heard their groaning and he remembered his covenant with Abraham, with Isaac and with Jacob. So God looked on the Israelites and was concerned about them.* **(Exodus 2:23–25)**

DAY 2

Spend some time writing and reflecting about what spoke to you in today's prayer reading.

THANKSGIVING AND PRAISE

Before you pray, spend some time listing what you are thankful for today and the ways that God is good.

PRAYER REQUESTS

What are the needs in your life, in your family, in your community, and in the world that you need to bring to God today? Make a list of those needs, and spend some time bringing each request before Him.

PRAYER PRACTICE REFLECTION

Today's prayer practice challenged you to simply sit before God in silence and allow Him to search your heart. As you opened your emotions to God, what did you find? Write about your experience and how it can change your approach to spending time with Him.

DAY 3

PRAY FOR THE IMPOSSIBLE

PRAYER READING (*LECTIO DIVINA*): Exodus 14

As you read and thoughtfully pray through today's selected Scripture, ask God to point out what He wants to teach you from His Word.

> *The Lord said to Moses, "Stretch out your hand over the sea so that the waters may flow back over the Egyptians and their chariots and horsemen." Moses stretched out his hand over the sea, and at daybreak the sea went back to its place. The Egyptians were fleeing toward it, and the Lord swept them into the sea. The water flowed back and covered the chariots and horsemen—the entire army of Pharaoh that had followed the Israelites into the sea. Not one of them survived. But the Israelites went through the sea on dry ground,*

> *with a wall of water on their right and on their left. That day the LORD saved Israel from the hands of the Egyptians, and Israel saw the Egyptians lying dead on the shore.*
> **(Exodus 14:26–30)**

Spend some time writing and reflecting about what spoke to you in today's prayer reading.

DAY 3

THANKSGIVING AND PRAISE

Before you pray, spend some time listing what you are thankful for today and the ways that God is good.

PRAYER REQUESTS

What are the needs in your life, in your family, in your community, and in the world that you need to bring to God today? Make a list of those needs, and spend some time bringing each request before Him.

PRAYER PRACTICE REFLECTION

The prayer practice challenged you to pray for people in your family, in your neighborhood, or in the world who may be facing impossible moments. How did this make you feel today? Who did God bring to mind for you and why? How can you further encourage them?

DAY 3

DAY 4

PRAYER AS PRAISE AND THANKSGIVING

PRAYER READING (***LECTIO DIVINA***): Exodus 15

As you read and thoughtfully pray through today's selected Scripture, ask God to point out what He wants to teach you from His Word.

> *Miriam the prophet, Aaron's sister, took a timbrel in her hand, and all the women followed her, with timbrels and dancing. Miriam sang to them: "Sing to the Lord, for he is highly exalted. Both horse and driver he has hurled into the sea."*
> **(Exodus 15:20–21)**

DAY 4

Spend some time writing and reflecting about what spoke to you in today's prayer reading.

THANKSGIVING AND PRAISE

Before you pray, spend some time listing what you are thankful for today and the ways that God is good.

PRAYER REQUESTS

What are the needs in your life, in your family, in your community, and in the world that you need to bring to God today? Make a list of those needs, and spend some time bringing each request before Him.

PRAYER PRACTICE REFLECTION

The prayer practice was to focus specifically on gratitude and thanksgiving, which is something we try to do every day in this journal. How did praying prayers of thanksgiving affect you? Did it bring joy to your day? Write about your experience.

DAY 5

PRAY EXPECTING TO SEE GOD'S GLORY

PRAYER READING (*LECTIO DIVINA*): Exodus 33

As you read and thoughtfully pray through today's selected Scripture, ask God to point out what He wants to teach you from His Word.

> *"How will anyone know that you are pleased with me and with your people unless you go with us? What else will distinguish me and your people from all the other people on the face of the earth?" And the Lord said to Moses, "I will do the very thing you have asked, because I am pleased with you and I know you by name." Then Moses said, "Now show me your glory." And the Lord said, "I will cause all my goodness to pass in front of you, and I will proclaim my*

> *name, the Lord, in your presence. I will have mercy on whom I will have mercy, and I will have compassion on whom I will have compassion. But," he said, "you cannot see my face, for no one may see me and live." Then the Lord said, "There is a place near me where you may stand on a rock. When my glory passes by, I will put you in a cleft in the rock and cover you with my hand until I have passed by. Then I will remove my hand and you will see my back; but my face must not be seen."* **(Exodus 33:16–23)**

Spend some time writing and reflecting about what spoke to you in today's prayer reading.

DAY 5

THANKSGIVING AND PRAISE

Before you pray, spend some time listing what you are thankful for today and the ways that God is good.

PRAYER REQUESTS

What are the needs in your life, in your family, in your community, and in the world that you need to bring to God today? Make a list of those needs, and spend some time bringing each request before Him.

PRAYER PRACTICE REFLECTION

In today's prayer practice, you wrote down some stories about God's faithfulness in your life along with some big challenges you may be facing. Sometimes it is helpful to consider how God has been faithful to others in our neighborhood, family, or community. Write about some times you have seen God's faithfulness in the lives of others. Spend a few moments thinking of other stories in the Bible where God was faithful, and write those down as a reminder that God can come through for you.

DAY 5

DAY 6

PRAYER BREAKS DOWN WALLS

PRAYER READING (*LECTIO DIVINA*): Joshua 5:13–6:20

As you read and thoughtfully pray through today's selected Scripture, ask God to point out what He wants to teach you from His Word.

> *When Joshua was near Jericho, he looked up and saw a man standing in front of him with a drawn sword in his hand. Joshua went up to him and asked, "Are you for us or for our enemies?" "Neither," he replied, "but as commander of the army of the LORD I have now come." Then Joshua fell facedown to the ground in reverence, and asked him, "What message does my LORD have for his servant?" The commander of the LORD's army replied, "Take off your*

> *sandals, for the place where you are standing is holy." And Joshua did so. Now the gates of Jericho were securely barred because of the Israelites. No one went out and no one came in. Then the LORD said to Joshua, "See, I have delivered Jericho into your hands, along with its king and its fighting men."* **(Joshua 5:13–6:2)**

Spend some time writing and reflecting about what spoke to you in today's prayer reading.

THANKSGIVING AND PRAISE

Before you pray, spend some time listing what you are thankful for today and the ways that God is good.

PRAYER REQUESTS

What are the needs in your life, in your family, in your community, and in the world that you need to bring to God today? Make a list of those needs, and spend some time bringing each request before Him.

PRAYER PRACTICE REFLECTION

In today's prayer practice you spent some moments acknowledging that you are on holy ground this very moment despite whatever challenges you may be facing. Observe the world around you and remember that God is present with you here. Write down a list of all that you can notice that is truly sacred about life—from your very breath to the sunshine or the rain, even the smile of someone passing by.

DAY 7

GOD MEETS US WHERE WE ARE

PRAYER READING (*LECTIO DIVINA*): Judges 6

As you read and thoughtfully pray through today's selected Scripture, ask God to point out what He wants to teach you from His Word.

> *Gideon said to God, "If you will save Israel by my hand as you have promised—look, I will place a wool fleece on the threshing floor. If there is dew only on the fleece and all the ground is dry, then I will know that you will save Israel by my hand, as you said." And that is what happened. Gideon rose early the next day; he squeezed the fleece and wrung out the dew—a bowlful of water. Then Gideon said to God, "Do not be angry with me. Let me make just one more request.*

> *Allow me one more test with the fleece, but this time make the fleece dry and let the ground be covered with dew." That night God did so. Only the fleece was dry; all the ground was covered with dew.* **(Judges 6:36–40)**

Spend some time writing and reflecting about what spoke to you in today's prayer reading.

DAY 7

THANKSGIVING AND PRAISE

Before you pray, spend some time listing what you are thankful for today and the ways that God is good.

PRAYER REQUESTS

What are the needs in your life, in your family, in your community, and in the world that you need to bring to God today? Make a list of those needs, and spend some time bringing each request before Him.

PRAYER PRACTICE REFLECTION

Today you spent time praying specifically about one door you believe God is calling you to step through. Write about that experience.

DAY 7

DAY 8

PRAY WITH HONESTY AND TRANSPARENCY

Prayer Reading (*Lectio Divina*): 1 Samuel 1:1–20

As you read and thoughtfully pray through today's selected Scripture, ask God to point out what He wants to teach you from His Word.

> *In her deep anguish Hannah prayed to the Lord, weeping bitterly. And she made a vow, saying, "Lord Almighty, if you will only look on your servant's misery and remember me, and not forget your servant but give her a son, then I will give him to the Lord for all the days of his life." . . . So in the course of time Hannah became pregnant and gave birth to a son. She named him Samuel, saying, "Because I asked the Lord for him"* **(1 Samuel 1:10–11, 20)**.

Spend some time writing and reflecting about what spoke to you in today's prayer reading.

THANKSGIVING AND PRAISE

Before you pray, spend some time listing what you are thankful for today and the ways that God is good.

DAY 8

PRAYER REQUESTS

What are the needs in your life, in your family, in your community, and in the world that you need to bring to God today? Make a list of those needs, and spend some time bringing each request before Him.

PRAYER PRACTICE REFLECTION

You were challenged to spend some time talking as honestly as you can to God. He knows all that is on your heart. Trust Him with your emotions today. Write about your experience of being more transparent with God. How did it make you feel closer to Him?

DAY 9

HEAR GOD'S GENTLE WHISPER

PRAYER READING (*LECTIO DIVINA*): 1 Kings 19

As you read and thoughtfully pray through today's selected Scripture, ask God to point out what He wants to teach you from His Word.

> *[Elijah] replied, "I have been very zealous for the Lord God Almighty. The Israelites have rejected your covenant, torn down your altars, and put your prophets to death with the sword. I am the only one left, and now they are trying to kill me too." The Lord said, "Go out and stand on the mountain in the presence of the Lord, for the Lord is about to pass by." Then a great and powerful wind tore the mountains apart and shattered the rocks before the Lord, but the Lord was*

> *not in the wind. After the wind there was an earthquake, but the LORD was not in the earthquake. After the earthquake came a fire, but the LORD was not in the fire. And after the fire came a gentle whisper.* **(1 Kings 19:10–13)**

Spend some time writing and reflecting about what spoke to you in today's prayer reading.

DAY 9

THANKSGIVING AND PRAISE

Before you pray, spend some time listing what you are thankful for today and the ways that God is good.

PRAYER REQUESTS

What are the needs in your life, in your family, in your community, and in the world that you need to bring to God today? Make a list of those needs, and spend some time bringing each request before Him.

PRAYER PRACTICE REFLECTION

In your prayer practice you found a quiet space to commit ten minutes of your day to listening for God's voice. Write about that experience and what you heard from God in that time of silence.

DAY 9

DAY 10

PRAY WHEN YOU'RE SURROUNDED AND HOPELESS

Prayer Reading (*Lectio Divina*): 2 Kings 6:8–22

As you read and thoughtfully pray through today's selected Scripture, ask God to point out what He wants to teach you from His Word.

> *When the servant of the man of God got up and went out early the next morning, an army with horses and chariots had surrounded the city. "Oh no, my lord! What shall we do?" the servant asked. "Don't be afraid," the prophet answered. "Those who are with us are more than those who are with them." And Elisha prayed, "Open his eyes, LORD, so that he*

> *may see." Then the LORD opened the servant's eyes, and he looked and saw the hills full of horses and chariots of fire all around Elisha. As the enemy came down toward him, Elisha prayed to the LORD, "Strike this army with blindness." So he struck them with blindness, as Elisha had asked.*
> **(2 Kings 6:15–18)**

Spend some time writing and reflecting about what spoke to you in today's prayer reading.

THANKSGIVING AND PRAISE

Before you pray, spend some time listing what you are thankful for today and the ways that God is good.

PRAYER REQUESTS

What are the needs in your life, in your family, in your community, and in the world that you need to bring to God today? Make a list of those needs, and spend some time bringing each request before Him.

PRAYER PRACTICE REFLECTION

As you spent time in prayer today asking God to open your eyes to His work in your life, your neighborhood, and your community, what did He bring to your attention? Write about the places where you need to be more awake to his presence and aware of what He is doing.

DAY 11

PRAY FOR PHYSICAL HEALING

PRAYER READING (*LECTIO DIVINA*): 2 Kings 20:1–11

As you read and thoughtfully pray through today's selected Scripture, ask God to point out what He wants to teach you from His Word.

> *In those days Hezekiah became ill and was at the point of death. The prophet Isaiah son of Amoz went to him and said, "This is what the LORD says: Put your house in order, because you are going to die; you will not recover." Hezekiah turned his face to the wall and prayed to the LORD, "Remember, LORD, how I have walked before you faithfully and with wholehearted devotion and have done what is good in your eyes." And Hezekiah wept bitterly. Before Isaiah had left the*

> *middle court, the word of the* L*ORD came to him: "Go back and tell Hezekiah, the ruler of my people, 'This is what the* L*ORD, the God of your father David, says: I have heard your prayer and seen your tears; I will heal you.'"* **(2 Kings 20:1–5)**

Spend some time writing and reflecting about what spoke to you in today's prayer reading.

DAY 11

THANKSGIVING AND PRAISE

Before you pray, spend some time listing what you are thankful for today and the ways that God is good.

PRAYER REQUESTS

What are the needs in your life, in your family, in your community, and in the world that you need to bring to God today? Make a list of those needs, and spend some time bringing each request before Him.

PRAYER PRACTICE REFLECTION

Today's practice asked you to make a list of those in your life or in your church community who need physical healing or to call someone who needs healing today and pray with them. Write about this prayer experience. What did you learn from it? How did God speak to you through this faithful prayer for healing?

DAY 11

DAY 12

PRAYER ALIGNS OUR DESIRES WITH GOD'S

PRAYER READING (*LECTIO DIVINA*): 2 Chronicles 1

As you read and thoughtfully pray through today's selected Scripture, ask God to point out what He wants to teach you from His Word.

> *"Now, Lord God, let your promise to my father David be confirmed, for you have made me king over a people who are as numerous as the dust of the earth. Give me wisdom and knowledge, that I may lead this people, for who is able to govern this great people of yours?" God said to Solomon, "Since this is your heart's desire and you have not asked for wealth, possessions or honor, nor for the death of your enemies, and since you have not asked for a long life but for*

> *wisdom and knowledge to govern my people over whom I have made you king, therefore wisdom and knowledge will be given you. And I will also give you wealth, possessions and honor, such as no king who was before you ever had and none after you will have."* **(2 Chronicles 1:9–12)**

Spend some time writing and reflecting about what spoke to you in today's prayer reading.

THANKSGIVING AND PRAISE

Before you pray, spend some time listing what you are thankful for today and the ways that God is good.

PRAYER REQUESTS

What are the needs in your life, in your family, in your community, and in the world that you need to bring to God today? Make a list of those needs, and spend some time bringing each request before Him.

PRAYER PRACTICE REFLECTION

Today you spent time considering the things God is calling you to do right now and asking Him to provide you with the specific tools you need to accomplish His will in your life. What came to mind as you prayed for guidance? How will God equip you to accomplish His will? Write down the things God brought to your attention during this time of prayer.

DAY 13

PRAY FOR GOD'S PROTECTION

PRAYER READING (*LECTIO DIVINA*): 2 Chronicles 14

As you read and thoughtfully pray through today's selected Scripture, ask God to point out what He wants to teach you from His Word.

> *Zerah the Cushite marched out against them with an army of thousands upon thousands and three hundred chariots, and came as far as Mareshah. Asa went out to meet him, and they took up battle positions in the Valley of Zephathah near Mareshah. Then Asa called to the LORD his God and said, "LORD, there is no one like you to help the powerless against the mighty. Help us, LORD our God, for we rely on you, and in your name, we have come against this vast army. LORD, you*

> *are our God; do not let mere mortals prevail against you."*
> *The LORD struck down the Cushites before Asa and Judah.*
> *The Cushites fled."* **(2 Chronicles 14:9–12)**

Spend some time writing and reflecting about what spoke to you in today's prayer reading.

DAY 13

THANKSGIVING AND PRAISE

Before you pray, spend some time listing what you are thankful for today and the ways that God is good.

PRAYER REQUESTS

What are the needs in your life, in your family, in your community, and in the world that you need to bring to God today? Make a list of those needs, and spend some time bringing each request before Him.

PRAYER PRACTICE REFLECTION

Today's practice challenged you to visualize God winning a battle for you. You wrote down in your journal what it will feel like when God brings peace and victory to your struggles. Now spend a few moments considering the ways that God's victory in your life could positively affect your family, your neighborhood, and your community.

DAY 13

DAY 14

PRAY FOR GOD'S BLESSING ON YOUR LIFE

PRAYER READING (*LECTIO DIVINA*): 1 Chronicles 4:1–10

As you read and thoughtfully pray through today's selected Scripture, ask God to point out what He wants to teach you from His Word.

> *Jabez was more honorable than his brothers. His mother had named him Jabez, saying, "I gave birth to him in pain." Jabez cried out to the God of Israel, "Oh, that you would bless me and enlarge my territory! Let your hand be with me, and keep me from harm so that I will be free from pain." And God granted his request.* **(1 Chronicles 4:9–10)**

DAY 14

Spend some time writing and reflecting about what spoke to you in today's prayer reading.

THANKSGIVING AND PRAISE

Before you pray, spend some time listing what you are thankful for today and the ways that God is good.

PRAYER REQUESTS

What are the needs in your life, in your family, in your community, and in the world that you need to bring to God today? Make a list of those needs, and spend some time bringing each request before Him.

PRAYER PRACTICE REFLECTION

In your prayer practice you wrote down a blessing on a note as a reminder of what God will do in your life. Blessings so often begin with gratitude. Look back at the list of things in today's journal that you are grateful for—many of them are simply unasked-for gifts that God has provided in your life. Write a thank-you note to God for these blessings.

ON OUR KNEES JOURNAL

DAY 15

PRAY WITH ASSURANCE

PRAYER READING (*LECTIO DIVINA*): 2 Chronicles 20

As you read and thoughtfully pray through today's selected Scripture, ask God to point out what He wants to teach you from His Word.

> *[Jahaziel] said: "Listen, King Jehoshaphat and all who live in Judah and Jerusalem! This is what the LORD says to you: 'Do not be afraid or discouraged because of this vast army. For the battle is not yours, but God's. Tomorrow march down against them. They will be climbing up by the Pass of Ziz, and you will find them at the end of the gorge in the Desert of Jeruel. You will not have to fight this battle. Take up your positions; stand firm and see the deliverance the LORD will give you, Judah and Jerusalem. Do not be afraid;*

> *do not be discouraged. Go out to face them tomorrow, and the LORD will be with you.'" Jehoshaphat bowed down with his face to the ground, and all the people of Judah and Jerusalem fell down in worship before the LORD. Then some Levites from the Kohathites and Korahites stood up and praised the LORD, the God of Israel, with a very loud voice.*
> **(2 Chronicles 20:15–19)**

Spend some time writing and reflecting about what spoke to you in today's prayer reading.

DAY 15

THANKSGIVING AND PRAISE

Before you pray, spend some time listing what you are thankful for today and the ways that God is good.

PRAYER REQUESTS

What are the needs in your life, in your family, in your community, and in the world that you need to bring to God today? Make a list of those needs, and spend some time bringing each request before Him.

PRAYER PRACTICE REFLECTION

Your prayer practice today challenged you to embrace the truth that no matter what you are facing, God will fight the battle for you. Spend some time writing about what your life will look like when God wins your battles.

DAY 15

DAY 16

PRAY FOR GOD'S PURPOSE

PRAYER READING (*LECTIO DIVINA*): Nehemiah 1

As you read and thoughtfully pray through today's selected Scripture, ask God to point out what He wants to teach you from His Word.

> *"Remember the instruction you gave your servant Moses, saying, 'If you are unfaithful, I will scatter you among the nations, but if you return to me and obey my commands, then even if your exiled people are at the farthest horizon, I will gather them from there and bring them to the place I have chosen as a dwelling for my Name.' They are your servants and your people, whom you redeemed by your great strength and your mighty hand. Lord, let your ear be attentive to the prayer of this your servant and to the prayer*

> *of your servants who delight in revering your name. Give your servant success today by granting him favor in the presence of this man."* **(Nehemiah 1:8–11)**

Spend some time writing and reflecting about what spoke to you in today's prayer reading.

THANKSGIVING AND PRAISE

Before you pray, spend some time listing what you are thankful for today and the ways that God is good.

PRAYER REQUESTS

What are the needs in your life, in your family, in your community, and in the world that you need to bring to God today? Make a list of those needs, and spend some time bringing each request before Him.

PRAYER PRACTICE REFLECTION

In today's practice you came to prayer focused on confession and repentance. (God no longer remembers your sins [Isaiah 43:25].) Write about what it means to you that you are truly released from your sins and burdens.

DAY 17

GOD HEARS US, EVEN IN OUR DISOBEDIENCE

Prayer Reading (*Lectio Divina*): Jonah 1–2

As you read and thoughtfully pray through today's selected Scripture, ask God to point out what He wants to teach you from His Word.

> *The LORD provided a huge fish to swallow Jonah, and Jonah was in the belly of the fish three days and three nights. . . . From inside the fish Jonah prayed to the LORD his God. . . . And the LORD commanded the fish, and it vomited Jonah onto dry land.* **(Jonah 1:17; 2:1; 2:10)**

Spend some time writing and reflecting about what spoke to you in today's prayer reading.

DAY 17

THANKSGIVING AND PRAISE

Before you pray, spend some time listing what you are thankful for today and the ways that God is good.

PRAYER REQUESTS

What are the needs in your life, in your family, in your community, and in the world that you need to bring to God today? Make a list of those needs, and spend some time bringing each request before Him

PRAYER PRACTICE REFLECTION

During prayer time you spent some moments asking God to help you trust Him more so you can experience the sense of peace and joy. Write about the areas where you struggle to trust God's faithfulness, and consider how you can surrender these areas to Him.

DAY 17

DAY 18

PRAY WITH SCRIPTURE

PRAYER READING (*LECTIO DIVINA*): Matthew 4:1–11

As you read and thoughtfully pray through today's selected Scripture, ask God to point out what He wants to teach you from His Word.

> *Then the devil took [Jesus] to the holy city and had him stand on the highest point of the temple. "If you are the Son of God," he said, "throw yourself down. For it is written: 'He will command his angels concerning you, and they will lift you up in their hands, so that you will not strike your foot against a stone.'" Jesus answered him, "It is also written: 'Do not put the Lord your God to the test.' Again, the devil took him to a very high mountain and showed him all the kingdoms of the world and their splendor. "All this I will give*

> *you," he said, "if you will bow down and worship me." Jesus said to him, "Away from me, Satan! For it is written: 'Worship the Lord your God and serve him only.'"* **(Matthew 4:5–10)**

Spend some time writing and reflecting about what spoke to you in today's prayer reading.

THANKSGIVING AND PRAISE

Before you pray, spend some time listing what you are thankful for today and the ways that God is good.

PRAYER REQUESTS

What are the needs in your life, in your family, in your community, and in the world that you need to bring to God today? Make a list of those needs, and spend some time bringing each request before Him.

PRAYER PRACTICE REFLECTION

As you have spent time meditating and praying over Scripture in this journal, how has it opened your heart to God's Word? Write about what you have learned in these past few days from your practice of praying the Scripture.

DAY 19

PRAY WITH SIMPLICITY

PRAYER READING (*LECTIO DIVINA*): Matthew 6

As you read and thoughtfully pray through today's selected Scripture, ask God to point out what He wants to teach you from His Word.

> *"When you pray, do not be like the hypocrites, for they love to pray standing in the synagogues and on the street corners to be seen by others. Truly I tell you, they have received their reward in full. But when you pray, go into your room, close the door and pray to your Father, who is unseen. Then your Father, who sees what is done in secret, will reward you. And when you pray, do not keep on babbling like pagans, for they think they will be heard because of their many words. Do not be like them, for your father knows what you need before you ask him."* **(Matthew 6:5–8)**

Spend some time writing and reflecting about what spoke to you in today's prayer reading.

DAY 19

THANKSGIVING AND PRAISE

Before you pray, spend some time listing what you are thankful for today and the ways that God is good.

PRAYER REQUESTS

What are the needs in your life, in your family, in your community, and in the world that you need to bring to God today? Make a list of those needs, and spend some time bringing each request before Him.

PRAYER PRACTICE REFLECTION

The prayer practice challenged you to find a quiet room, close the door, turn off your phone, and talk to God as honestly as you can about your life. Write about the experience of intentionally praying in this way and how it can affect your relationship with God.

DAY 19

DAY 20

PRAY TOGETHER!

PRAYER READING (*LECTIO DIVINA*): Matthew 18

As you read and thoughtfully pray through today's selected Scripture, ask God to point out what He wants to teach you from His Word.

> *"Truly I tell you, whatever you bind on earth will be bound in heaven, and whatever you loose on earth will be loosed in heaven. Again, truly I tell you that if two of you on earth agree about anything they ask for, it will be done for them by my Father in heaven. For where two or three gather in my name, there am I with them."* **(Matthew 18:18–20)**

DAY 20

Spend some time writing and reflecting about what spoke to you in today's prayer reading.

THANKSGIVING AND PRAISE

Before you pray, spend some time listing what you are thankful for today and the ways that God is good.

PRAYER REQUESTS

What are the needs in your life, in your family, in your community, and in the world that you need to bring to God today? Make a list of those needs, and spend some time bringing each request before Him.

PRAYER PRACTICE REFLECTION

Today's prayer practice challenged you to pray by gathering with others in your faith community (small group, church, or good friends). How can praying with other believers strengthen your faith? What did this prayer time remind you about God and about your prayer partners?

DAY 21

PRAY FOR THOSE WHO CANNOT (OR WILL NOT)

PRAYER READING (*LECTIO DIVINA*): Mark 2:1–12

As you read and thoughtfully pray through today's selected Scripture, ask God to point out what He wants to teach you from His Word.

> *A few days later, when Jesus again entered Capernaum, the people heard that he had come home. They gathered in such large numbers that there was no room left, not even outside the door, and he preached the word to them. Some men came, bringing to him a paralyzed man, carried by four of them. Since they could not get him to Jesus because of the crowd, they made an opening in the roof above Jesus by digging through it and then lowered the mat the man was*

> *lying on. When Jesus saw their faith, he said to the paralyzed man, "Son, your sins are forgiven."* **(Mark 2:1–5)**

Spend some time writing and reflecting about what spoke to you in today's prayer reading.

DAY 21

THANKSGIVING AND PRAISE

Before you pray, spend some time listing what you are thankful for today and the ways that God is good.

PRAYER REQUESTS

What are the needs in your life, in your family, in your community, and in the world that you need to bring to God today? Make a list of those needs, and spend some time bringing each request before Him.

PRAYER PRACTICE REFLECTION

As you were called to pray for others who need the healing or forgiveness of God today in your prayer practice, who came to mind? Write about these people and their situations, and ask God to show you the ways that you can reflect His love, grace, and healing in their lives (or situations).

DAY 21

DAY 22

PRAY WITHOUT FEAR

PRAYER READING (*LECTIO DIVINA*): Mark 5:21–43

As you read and thoughtfully pray through today's selected Scripture, ask God to point out what He wants to teach you from His Word.

> *One of the synagogue leaders, named Jairus, came, and when he saw Jesus, he fell at his feet. He pleaded earnestly with him, "My little daughter is dying. Please come and put your hands on her so that she will be healed and live." So Jesus went with him. . . . While Jesus was still speaking, some people came from the house of Jairus, the synagogue leader. "Your daughter is dead," they said. "Why bother the teacher anymore?" Overhearing what they said, Jesus told him, "Don't be afraid; just believe."* **(Mark 5:22–24, 35–36)**

DAY 22

Spend some time writing and reflecting about what spoke to you in today's prayer reading.

THANKSGIVING AND PRAISE

Before you pray, spend some time listing what you are thankful for today and the ways that God is good.

PRAYER REQUESTS

What are the needs in your life, in your family, in your community, and in the world that you need to bring to God today? Make a list of those needs, and spend some time bringing each request before Him.

PRAYER PRACTICE REFLECTION

Today you were asked to write down the fears that you are facing in your life right now, to pray over those fears and ask God to show you how to embrace belief instead of fear. Take your list of fears, and spend a few minutes writing about how practicing trust in God will change each situation.

DAY 23

PRAY WITH A HEART OF FORGIVENESS

PRAYER READING (*LECTIO DIVINA*): Mark 11

As you read and thoughtfully pray through today's selected Scripture, ask God to point out what He wants to teach you from His Word.

> *"Have faith in God," Jesus answered [Peter]. "Truly I tell you, if anyone says to this mountain, 'Go, throw yourself into the sea,' and does not doubt in their heart but believes that what they say will happen, it will be done for them. Therefore I tell you, whatever you ask for in prayer, believe that you have received it, and it will be yours. And when you stand praying, if you hold anything against anyone, forgive them,*

> *so that your Father in heaven may forgive you your sins."*
> **(Mark 11:22–25)**

Spend some time writing and reflecting about what spoke to you in today's prayer reading.

DAY 23

THANKSGIVING AND PRAISE

Before you pray, spend some time listing what you are thankful for today and the ways that God is good.

PRAYER REQUESTS

What are the needs in your life, in your family, in your community, and in the world that you need to bring to God today? Make a list of those needs, and spend some time bringing each request before Him.

PRAYER PRACTICE REFLECTION

You were challenged to make a list of people God wants you to forgive today. Write about that process and how you feel after this time of prayer and forgiveness. Consider how offering forgiveness as a part of prayer time can free you to experience the joy God has for you.

DAY 24

PRAY PATIENTLY—GOD'S TIMING IS PERFECT

PRAYER READING (*LECTIO DIVINA*): Luke 1

As you read and thoughtfully pray through today's selected Scripture, ask God to point out what He wants to teach you from His Word.

> *Then an angel of the Lord appeared to him, standing at the right side of the altar of incense. When Zechariah saw him, he was startled and was gripped with fear. But the angel said to him: "Do not be afraid, Zechariah; your prayer has been heard. Your wife Elizabeth will bear you a son, and you are to call him John. He will be a joy and delight to you, and many will rejoice because of his birth, for he will be great in the sight of the Lord. He is never to take wine or other fermented*

> *drink, and he will be filled with the Holy Spirit even before he is born."* **(Luke 1:11–15)**

Spend some time writing and reflecting about what spoke to you in today's prayer reading.

THANKSGIVING AND PRAISE

Before you pray, spend some time listing what you are thankful for today and the ways that God is good.

PRAYER REQUESTS

What are the needs in your life, in your family, in your community, and in the world that you need to bring to God today? Make a list of those needs, and spend some time bringing each request before Him.

PRAYER PRACTICE REFLECTION

In your prayer practice you were to write a list of three situations that you have been praying for and waiting on God's response. Spend some time writing and reflecting on what you have learned about God (and about yourself) as you have waited on Him in this season of prayer. In what ways have you grown during this season of waiting?

DAY 25

PRAY WITH HOPE AND ANTICIPATION

PRAYER READING (*LECTIO DIVINA*): Luke 8

As you read and thoughtfully pray through today's selected Scripture, ask God to point out what He wants to teach you from His Word.

> *A woman was there who had been subject to bleeding for twelve years, but no one could heal her. She came up behind him and touched the edge of his cloak, and immediately her bleeding stopped. "Who touched me?" Jesus asked. When they all denied it, Peter said, "Master, the people are crowding and pressing against you." But Jesus said, "Someone touched me; I know that power has gone out from me." Then the woman, seeing that she could not*

> *go unnoticed, came trembling and fell at his feet. In the presence of all the people, she told why she had touched him and how she had been instantly healed. Then he said to her, "Daughter, your faith has healed you. Go in peace."*
> **(Luke 8:43–48)**

Spend some time writing and reflecting about what spoke to you in today's prayer reading.

DAY 25

THANKSGIVING AND PRAISE

Before you pray, spend some time listing what you are thankful for today and the ways that God is good.

PRAYER REQUESTS

What are the needs in your life, in your family, in your community, and in the world that you need to bring to God today? Make a list of those needs, and spend some time bringing each request before Him.

PRAYER PRACTICE REFLECTION

Today you were asked to consider a desperate need that you have been hesitant to bring to God. As you prayed, you visualized reaching out and touching Jesus's robe and trusting him to deliver. Spend some time writing about this experience with imaginative prayer and how it affected you.

DAY 25

DAY 26

PRAY AS JESUS PRAYED

PRAYER READING (*LECTIO DIVINA*): Luke 11

As you read and thoughtfully pray through today's selected Scripture, ask God to point out what He wants to teach you from His Word.

> *One day Jesus was praying in a certain place. When he finished, one of his disciples said to him, "Lord, teach us to pray, just as John taught his disciples." He said to them, "When you pray, say: 'Father, hallowed be your name, your kingdom come. Give us each day our daily bread. Forgive us our sins, for we also forgive everyone who sins against us. And lead us not into temptation.'"* **(Luke 11:1–4)**

DAY 26

Spend some time writing and reflecting about what spoke to you in today's prayer reading.

THANKSGIVING AND PRAISE

Before you pray, spend some time listing what you are thankful for today and the ways that God is good.

PRAYER REQUESTS

What are the needs in your life, in your family, in your community, and in the world that you need to bring to God today? Make a list of those needs, and spend some time bringing each request before Him.

PRAYER PRACTICE REFLECTION

Today's prayer practice asked you to recite the Lord's Prayer throughout your day. Write about how God spoke to you through this practice. What did you notice today about the Lord's Prayer that maybe you had not before?

ON OUR KNEES JOURNAL

DAY 27

PRAY TO *THE* GOOD FATHER

Prayer Reading (*Lectio Divina*): Luke 11

As you read and thoughtfully pray through today's selected Scripture, ask God to point out what He wants to teach you from His Word.

> *"So I say to you: Ask and it will be given to you; seek and you will find; knock and the door will be opened to you. For everyone who asks receives; the one who seeks finds; and to the one who knocks, the door will be opened. "Which of you fathers, if your son asks for a fish, will give him a snake instead? Or if he asks for an egg, will give him a scorpion? If you then, though you are evil, know how to give good gifts to your children, how much more will your Father in heaven give the Holy Spirit to those who ask him!"* **(Luke 11:9–13)**

Spend some time writing and reflecting about what spoke to you in today's prayer reading.

DAY 27

THANKSGIVING AND PRAISE

Before you pray, spend some time listing what you are thankful for today and the ways that God is good.

PRAYER REQUESTS

What are the needs in your life, in your family, in your community, and in the world that you need to bring to God today? Make a list of those needs, and spend some time bringing each request before Him.

PRAYER PRACTICE REFLECTION

You began your prayer practice today by addressing God the way Jesus did, as "Abba Father." How does approaching God in prayer as your divine dad—the *good* father who cares about your every need—change your prayer time?

DAY 27

DAY 28

PRAY WITH PERSISTENCE

PRAYER READING (*LECTIO DIVINA*): Luke 18

As you read and thoughtfully pray through today's selected Scripture, ask God to point out what He wants to teach you from His Word.

> *Jesus told his disciples a parable to show them that they should always pray and not give up. He said: "In a certain town there was a judge who neither feared God nor cared what people thought. And there was a widow in that town who kept coming to him with the plea, 'Grant me justice against my adversary.' For some time, he refused. But finally, he said to himself, 'Even though I don't fear God or care what people think, yet because this widow keeps bothering me, I will see that she gets justice, so that she won't eventually come and attack me!'"* **(Luke 18:1–5)**.

DAY 28

Spend some time writing and reflecting about what spoke to you in today's prayer reading.

THANKSGIVING AND PRAISE

Before you pray, spend some time listing what you are thankful for today and the ways that God is good.

PRAYER REQUESTS

What are the needs in your life, in your family, in your community, and in the world that you need to bring to God today? Make a list of those needs, and spend some time bringing each request before Him.

PRAYER PRACTICE REFLECTION

In your prayer practice you shared some of the things that you find difficult to pray for with a friend, a small group, or a pastor. Write about the ways you can encourage others in your own community to pray with persistence even in the face of difficulty.

DAY 29

PRAY WITH HUMILITY

PRAYER READING (*LECTIO DIVINA*): Luke 18

As you read and thoughtfully pray through today's selected Scripture, ask God to point out what He wants to teach you from His Word.

> *To some who were confident of their own righteousness and looked down on everyone else, Jesus told this parable: "Two men went up to the temple to pray, one a Pharisee and the other a tax collector. The Pharisee stood by himself and prayed: 'God, I thank you that I am not like other people—robbers, evildoers, adulterers—or even like this tax collector. I fast twice a week and give a tenth of all I get.' But the tax collector stood at a distance. He would not even look up to heaven, but beat his breast and said, 'God, have mercy*

> *on me, a sinner.' I tell you that this man, rather than the other, went home justified before God. For all those who exalt themselves will be humbled, and those who humble themselves will be exalted."* **(Luke 18:9–14)**

Spend some time writing and reflecting about what spoke to you in today's prayer reading.

DAY 29

THANKSGIVING AND PRAISE

Before you pray, spend some time listing what you are thankful for today and the ways that God is good.

PRAYER REQUESTS

What are the needs in your life, in your family, in your community, and in the world that you need to bring to God today? Make a list of those needs, and spend some time bringing each request before Him.

PRAYER PRACTICE REFLECTION

In today's practice you asked God to show you the areas of your life where you need humility. Write about what God pointed out in this time of prayer and reflection and how you can surrender these areas to Him.

DAY 29

DAY 30

PRAY FOR STRENGTH IN TIMES OF DISTRESS

PRAYER READING (*LECTIO DIVINA*): Luke 22:39–46

As you read and thoughtfully pray through today's selected Scripture, ask God to point out what He wants to teach you from His Word.

> *[Jesus] withdrew about a stone's throw beyond them, knelt down and prayed, "Father, if you are willing, take this cup from me; yet not my will, but yours be done." An angel from heaven appeared to him and strengthened him. And being in anguish, he prayed more earnestly, and his sweat was like drops of blood falling to the ground.* **(Luke 22:41–44)**

DAY 30

Spend some time writing and reflecting about what spoke to you in today's prayer reading.

THANKSGIVING AND PRAISE

Before you pray, spend some time listing what you are thankful for today and the ways that God is good.

PRAYER REQUESTS

What are the needs in your life, in your family, in your community, and in the world that you need to bring to God today? Make a list of those needs, and spend some time bringing each request before Him.

PRAYER PRACTICE REFLECTION

Today's prayer practice asked you to go outside and spend some moments visualizing and meditating on the scene in Luke of Jesus praying in the garden to see what God wanted to teach you about prayer. Write about that experience.

DAY 31

PRAY AS THOUGH YOU BELONG

PRAYER READING (*LECTIO DIVINA*): Luke 23

As you read and thoughtfully pray through today's selected Scripture, ask God to point out what He wants to teach you from His Word.

> *One of the criminals who hung there hurled insults at him: "Aren't you the Messiah? Save yourself and us!" But the other criminal rebuked him. "Don't you fear God," he said, "since you are under the same sentence? We are punished justly, for we are getting what our deeds deserve. But this man has done nothing wrong." Then he said, "Jesus, remember me when you come into your kingdom." Jesus answered him, "Truly I tell you, today you will be with me in paradise."*
> **(Luke 23:39–43)**

Spend some time writing and reflecting about what spoke to you in today's prayer reading.

DAY 31

THANKSGIVING AND PRAISE

Before you pray, spend some time listing what you are thankful for today and the ways that God is good.

PRAYER REQUESTS

What are the needs in your life, in your family, in your community, and in the world that you need to bring to God today? Make a list of those needs, and spend some time bringing each request before Him.

PRAYER PRACTICE REFLECTION

You were challenged to spend time throughout your day today simply saying thank you to God whenever His grace comes to mind. Spend a few moments writing about what God's grace means to you in your life and the lives of the people in your family and community.

DAY 31

DAY 32

PRAY IN THE NAME OF JESUS

PRAYER READING (*LECTIO DIVINA*): John 14

As you read and thoughtfully pray through today's selected Scripture, ask God to point out what He wants to teach you from His Word.

> *"Don't you believe that I am in the Father, and that the Father is in me? The words I say to you I do not speak on my own authority. Rather, it is the Father, living in me, who is doing his work. Believe me when I say that I am in the Father and the Father is in me; or at least believe on the evidence of the works themselves. Very truly I tell you, whoever believes in me will do the works I have been doing, and they will do even greater things than these, because I am going to the Father. And I will do whatever you ask in my name, so that*

> *the Father may be glorified in the Son. You may ask me for anything in my name, and I will do it."* **(John 14:10–14)**

Spend some time writing and reflecting about what spoke to you in today's prayer reading.

THANKSGIVING AND PRAISE

Before you pray, spend some time listing what you are thankful for today and the ways that God is good.

PRAYER REQUESTS

What are the needs in your life, in your family, in your community, and in the world that you need to bring to God today? Make a list of those needs, and spend some time bringing each request before Him.

PRAYER PRACTICE REFLECTION

Today's practice challenged you to pray in Jesus's name and to be confident that your prayers will be answered. Write about what it means to you that Jesus promises this in John 14:14.

DAY 33

PRAY WITH THE HOLY SPIRIT

PRAYER READING (*LECTIO DIVINA*): Acts 2:1–13

As you read and thoughtfully pray through today's selected Scripture, ask God to point out what He wants to teach you from His Word.

> *When the day of Pentecost came, they were all together in one place. Suddenly a sound like the blowing of a violent wind came from heaven and filled the whole house where they were sitting. They saw what seemed to be tongues of fire that separated and came to rest on each of them. All of them were filled with the Holy Spirit and began to speak in other tongues as the Spirit enabled them. Now there were staying in Jerusalem God-fearing Jews from every nation*

> *under heaven. When they heard this sound, a crowd came together in bewilderment, because each one heard their own language being spoken.* **(Acts 2:1–6)**

Spend some time writing and reflecting about what spoke to you in today's prayer reading.

THANKSGIVING AND PRAISE

Before you pray, spend some time listing what you are thankful for today and the ways that God is good.

PRAYER REQUESTS

What are the needs in your life, in your family, in your community, and in the world that you need to bring to God today? Make a list of those needs, and spend some time bringing each request before Him.

PRAYER PRACTICE REFLECTION

Today you spent some time inviting the Holy Spirit to be present in your prayer time, and you asked for whom and for what you should pray. Spend some time writing and reflecting about that experience.

DAY 33

DAY 34

PRAY WITH BOLDNESS

PRAYER READING (*LECTIO DIVINA*): Acts 4

As you read and thoughtfully pray through today's selected Scripture, ask God to point out what He wants to teach you from His Word.

> *"Now, Lord, consider their threats and enable your servants to speak your word with great boldness. Stretch out your hand to heal and perform signs and wonders through the name of your holy servant Jesus." After they prayed, the place where they were meeting was shaken. And they were all filled with the Holy Spirit and spoke the word of God boldly. All the believers were one in heart and mind. No one claimed that any of their possessions was their own, but they shared everything they had. With great power the apostles*

> *continued to testify to the resurrection of the Lord Jesus. And God's grace was so powerfully at work in them all.*
> **(Acts 4:29–33)**

Spend some time writing and reflecting about what spoke to you in today's prayer reading.

THANKSGIVING AND PRAISE

Before you pray, spend some time listing what you are thankful for today and the ways that God is good.

PRAYER REQUESTS

What are the needs in your life, in your family, in your community, and in the world that you need to bring to God today? Make a list of those needs, and spend some time bringing each request before Him.

PRAYER PRACTICE REFLECTION

Today in the prayer practice you asked the Holy Spirit to give you boldness where you need it most. Spend some time writing and reflecting on how you can begin to take action and be bolder in your faith in those specific areas of your life.

ON OUR KNEES JOURNAL

DAY 35

PRAY FOR OUR ENEMIES

PRAYER READING (*LECTIO DIVINA*): Acts 7

As you read and thoughtfully pray through today's selected Scripture, ask God to point out what He wants to teach you from His Word.

> *When the members of the Sanhedrin heard this, they were furious and gnashed their teeth at him. But Stephen, full of the Holy Spirit, looked up to heaven and saw the glory of God, and Jesus standing at the right hand of God. "Look," he said, "I see heaven open and the Son of Man standing at the right hand of God." At this they covered their ears and, yelling at the top of their voices, they all rushed at him, dragged him out of the city and began to stone him. Meanwhile, the witnesses laid their coats at the feet of*

> *a young man named Saul. While they were stoning him, Stephen prayed, "Lord Jesus, receive my spirit." Then he fell on his knees and cried out, "Lord, do not hold this sin against them." When he had said this, he fell asleep.* **(Acts 7:54–60)**

Spend some time writing and reflecting about what spoke to you in today's prayer reading.

THANKSGIVING AND PRAISE

Before you pray, spend some time listing what you are thankful for today and the ways that God is good.

PRAYER REQUESTS

What are the needs in your life, in your family, in your community, and in the world that you need to bring to God today? Make a list of those needs, and spend some time bringing each request before Him.

PRAYER PRACTICE REFLECTION

Today's practice asked you to make a private list of the people who have hurt you. You committed to praying for each of them and embracing the freedom God offers in forgiveness. (Remember that forgiveness never requires you to return to people or situations that may be harmful to you.) Take a moment to write and reflect about this experience. What was challenging? Did it help you begin to feel any sense freedom?

DAY 35

DAY 36

PRAY FOR GOD TO RESCUE OTHERS

PRAYER READING (*LECTIO DIVINA*): Acts 12

As you read and thoughtfully pray through today's selected Scripture, ask God to point out what He wants to teach you from His Word.

> *It was about this time that King Herod arrested some who belonged to the church, intending to persecute them. He had James, the brother of John, put to death with the sword. When he saw that this met with approval among the Jews, he proceeded to seize Peter also. This happened during the Festival of Unleavened Bread. After arresting him, he put him in prison, handing him over to be guarded by four squads of four soldiers each. Herod intended to bring him*

> *out for public trial after the Passover. So, Peter was kept in prison, but the church was earnestly praying to God for him. The night before Herod was to bring him to trial, Peter was sleeping between two soldiers, bound with two chains, and sentries stood guard at the entrance. Suddenly an angel of the Lord appeared and a light shone in the cell. He struck Peter on the side and woke him up. "Quick, get up!" he said, and the chains fell off Peter's wrists.* **(Acts 12:1–7)**

Spend some time writing and reflecting about what spoke to you in today's prayer reading.

THANKSGIVING AND PRAISE

Before you pray, spend some time listing what you are thankful for today and the ways that God is good.

PRAYER REQUESTS

What are the needs in your life, in your family, in your community, and in the world that you need to bring to God today? Make a list of those needs, and spend some time bringing each request before Him.

PRAYER PRACTICE REFLECTION

Today you committed to praying for your neighbors. You made a list and posted it somewhere prominent as a reminder. Take a moment in this journal to write down specifically how you are praying for God to move in the lives of each of the people on your list.

DAY 37

PRAYER IS YOUR PATH TO FREEDOM

PRAYER READING (*LECTIO DIVINA*): Acts 16:16–38

As you read and thoughtfully pray through today's selected Scripture, ask God to point out what He wants to teach you from His Word.

> *After [Paul and Silas] had been severely flogged, they were thrown into prison, and the jailer was commanded to guard them carefully. When he received these orders, he put them in the inner cell and fastened their feet in the stocks. About midnight Paul and Silas were praying and singing hymns to God, and the other prisoners were listening to them. Suddenly there was such a violent earthquake that the foundations of the prison were shaken. At once all the prison doors flew open, and everyone's chains came loose.*
> **(Acts 16:23–26)**

Spend some time writing and reflecting about what spoke to you in today's prayer reading.

DAY 37

THANKSGIVING AND PRAISE

Before you pray, spend some time listing what you are thankful for today and the ways that God is good.

PRAYER REQUESTS

What are the needs in your life, in your family, in your community, and in the world that you need to bring to God today? Make a list of those needs, and spend some time bringing each request before Him.

PRAYER PRACTICE REFLECTION

Today you spent a few moments thinking of the people who are imprisoned in illness or addiction, and you prayed for them specifically. Now spend a few moments reflecting about the areas of your own life where you feel imprisoned, under attack, or weighed down. Ask God to shake the very foundations of those situations in your life today.

DAY 37

DAY 38

PRAYER WILL EXCEED OUR EXPECTATIONS

PRAYER READING (*LECTIO DIVINA*): Ephesians 3

As you read and thoughtfully pray through today's selected Scripture, ask God to point out what He wants to teach you from His Word.

> *I pray that out of his glorious riches he may strengthen you with power through his Spirit in your inner being, so that Christ may dwell in your hearts through faith. And I pray that you, being rooted and established in love, may have power, together with all the Lord's holy people, to grasp how wide and long and high and deep is the love of Christ, and to know this love that surpasses knowledge—that you may be filled to the measure of all the fullness of God. Now to him who can*

> *do immeasurably more than all we ask or imagine, according to his power that is at work within us, to him be glory in the church and in Christ Jesus throughout all generations, for ever and ever! Amen.* **(Ephesians 3:16–21)**

Spend some time writing and reflecting about what spoke to you in today's prayer reading.

THANKSGIVING AND PRAISE

Before you pray, spend some time listing what you are thankful for today and the ways that God is good.

PRAYER REQUESTS

What are the needs in your life, in your family, in your community, and in the world that you need to bring to God today? Make a list of those needs, and spend some time bringing each request before Him.

PRAYER PRACTICE REFLECTION

Today you spent time praising God for the amazing work He had done and is still doing in your life. Write and reflect on what that meant to you. How does simply focusing on praise during prayer affect you? What is different about the experience?

ON OUR KNEES JOURNAL

DAY 39

PRAYER AS SPIRITUAL WARFARE

PRAYER READING (*LECTIO DIVINA*): Ephesians 6

As you read and thoughtfully pray through today's selected Scripture, ask God to point out what He wants to teach you from His Word.

> *Be strong in the Lord and in his mighty power. Put on the full armor of God, so that you can take your stand against the devil's schemes. For our struggle is not against flesh and blood, but against the rulers, against the authorities, against the powers of this dark world and against the spiritual forces of evil in the heavenly realms. Therefore put on the full armor of God, so that when the day of evil comes, you may be able to stand your ground, and after you have done everything, to*

> *stand. Stand firm then, with the belt of truth buckled around your waist, with the breastplate of righteousness in place, and with your feet fitted with the readiness that comes from the gospel of peace. In addition to all this, take up the shield of faith, with which you can extinguish all the flaming arrows of the evil one. Take the helmet of salvation and the sword of the Spirit, which is the word of God. And pray in the Spirit on all occasions with all kinds of prayers and requests. With this in mind, be alert and always keep on praying for all the Lord's people.* **(Ephesians 6:10–18)**

Spend some time writing and reflecting about what spoke to you in today's prayer reading.

THANKSGIVING AND PRAISE

Before you pray, spend some time listing what you are thankful for today and the ways that God is good.

PRAYER REQUESTS

What are the needs in your life, in your family, in your community, and in the world that you need to bring to God today? Make a list of those needs, and spend some time bringing each request before Him.

PRAYER PRACTICE REFLECTION

Today you were asked to consider the ways God has equipped you to get into the spiritual fight and empowered you to love and serve others. Write and reflect on the ways that God is calling you to love and serve these specific people.

DAY 39

DAY 40

PRAY WITHOUT ANXIETY

PRAYER READING (*LECTIO DIVINA*): Philippians 4

As you read and thoughtfully pray through today's selected Scripture, ask God to point out what He wants to teach you from His Word.

> *Do not be anxious about anything, but in every situation, by prayer and petition, with thanksgiving, present your requests to God. And the peace of God, which transcends all understanding, will guard your hearts and your minds in Christ Jesus.* **(Philippians 4:6–7)**

DAY 40

Spend some time writing and reflecting about what spoke to you in today's prayer reading.

THANKSGIVING AND PRAISE

Before you pray, spend some time listing what you are thankful for today and the ways that God is good.

PRAYER REQUESTS

What are the needs in your life, in your family, in your community, and in the world that you need to bring to God today? Make a list of those needs, and spend some time bringing each request before Him.

PRAYER PRACTICE REFLECTION

Today you took a few moments before you prayed just to breathe. As you breathed in and out for several moments, you began by thanking God for your very breath. Write and reflect on the ways that focusing on just being grateful to God for something as simple as your breath can remind you of his faithful love.

ON OUR KNEES JOURNAL

ON OUR KNEES JOURNAL

ON OUR KNEES JOURNAL

ABOUT THE AUTHOR

Since his self-titled debut in 2006, Phil Wickham has emerged as a leader in the modern worship movement, penning countless songs sung in churches around the world. His RIAA Gold®-certified single, "This Is Amazing Grace," was his first career No. 1, holding the top spot for thirteen consecutive weeks and named *Billboard*'s No. 1 Christian Airplay Song of the Year in 2014 and BMI's Christian Song of the Year in 2015. His anthemic "Living Hope," also RIAA Gold-certified, earned him a GMA Dove Award for Worship Recorded Song of the Year in 2019.

His latest project, *Hymn of Heaven* (June 25, 2021, Fair Trade Services), was written during a year when the family of God couldn't physically gather in houses of worship around the world. "*Hymn of Heaven* is full of praise and thankfulness, just lifting up the name of Jesus and speaking what we really know the reality is even though we don't see it," he says. "All I want to do is facilitate moments where people can encounter the presence of God." The album's first single, "Battle Belongs," had already topped five different radio charts for multiple weeks.

Wickham's music has received hundreds of millions of streams across his catalog and platforms, with his discography including eight full-length projects, multiple Christmas releases, and a series of popular *Singalong* records that capture Wickham's songs doing what they were always meant to do—giving people language to sing to God. To find out more, visit PhilWickham.com.

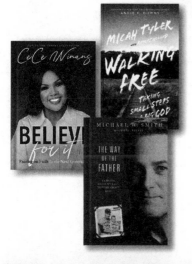

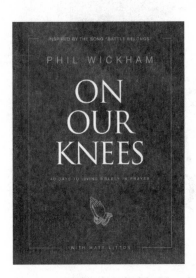

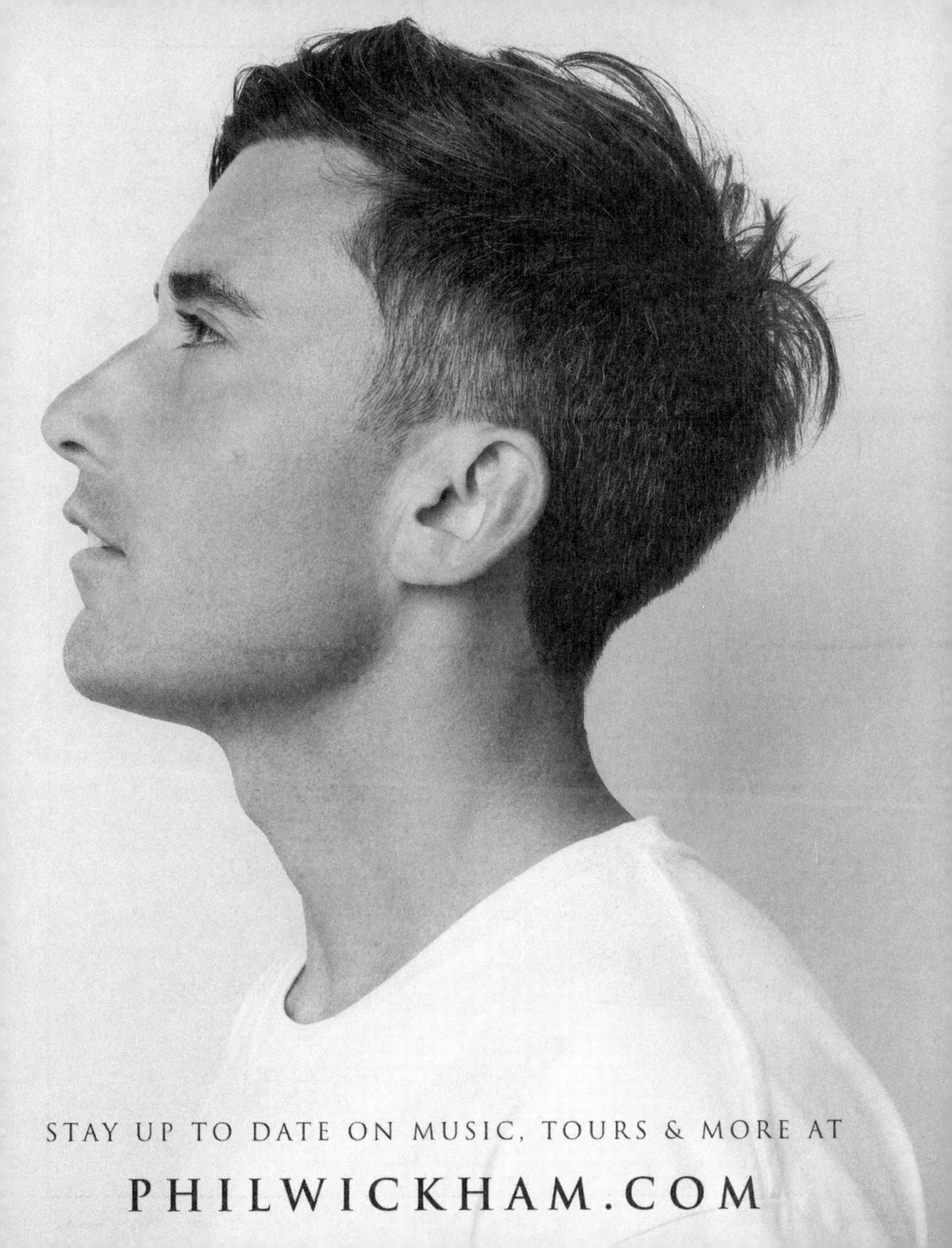
STAY UP TO DATE ON MUSIC, TOURS & MORE AT
PHILWICKHAM.COM